Also by Andrew Mossin

POETRY & CHAPBOOKS

Drafts for Shelley

From Blake's Notebook

The Epochal Body

The Veil

Exile's Recital

Torture Papers

Stanzas for the Preparation of Perception

The Fire Cycle

North & East: Daybooks

Black Trees

MEMOIR

A Son from the Mountains

CRITICISM

Male Subjectivity and Poetic Form in "New American" Poetry

Thinking with the Poem:

Essays on the Poetry and Poetics of Rachel Blau DuPlessis

Whitman
At The Bardo

Andrew Mossin

SPUYTEN DUYVIL
New York City

Library of Congress Control Number: 2025931204

Images herein are from:

Whitman, Walt. "Last of ebb, and daylight waning." The Walt Whitman Archive. Gen. ed. Matt Cohen, Ed Folsom, & Kenneth M. Price. Accessed 31 December 2024. <http://www.whitmanarchive.org>.

Whitman, Walt. "cottonwood." The Walt Whitman Archive. Gen. ed. Matt Cohen, Ed Folsom, & Kenneth M. Price. Accessed 31 December 2024. <http://www.whitmanarchive.org>.

Whitman, Walt. "This is the Earths word." The Walt Whitman Archive. Gen. ed. Matt Cohen, Ed Folsom, & Kenneth M. Price. Accessed 31 December 2024. <http://www.whitmanarchive.org>.

https://upload.wikimedia.org/wikipedia/commons/9/95/Dwight_William_Tryon_-_Moonrise_-_23.11_-_Indianapolis_Museum_of_Art.jpg

For Peter O'Leary

'The dead do read us....'
Letter to John Taggart

<del>I Last of the ebb, and daylight</del>
Poured out

Last of ebb, and daylight *waning,*
Scented sea-breaths landward making —
 smells of sedge and salt incoming,
With many a half-caught voice sent
 up from the whirls and eddies.
Many a muffled confession — many a
 sob and whisper'd word,
As from speakers far or hid.

How they sweep down and out! how they mutter!
Heroes unnamed — poets and artists, greatest of any,
Pride of manhood, tones of the dying
Tones of the dying — a chorus of age's complaints —
 — love unreturn'd — hope's last words,
Some suicide's despair'd beguiling cry. Away
 to the boundless waste, and never
 again return.

On to oblivion then! on quicker yet!
 on — on, and do your part, ye shrouding waters!
On, for your time, ye furious debouché!

I

Of all the plenty ~~in nature~~ there is, no plenty is comparable to the plenty of time and space.—Of these there is ample store,— there is no limit

Whitman, Notebooks

Neither birth nor death
but heaven's third

door
that startles by its

sudden appearance
here   in the middle of

day…

Habitat releasing its colors
to the world

turquoise and cinnamon
blended

seen partially

out one's half-shut
eye.

*

'Home again—down
in the country, absorbing

perfect nights and days.'

To clean the body is to erase
its wants

to come from nothing
outside or in

one day at a time.

*

Yet how say the work is
beginning, little or

nothing, a gift
brought to the table—

'I speak little or nothing; I
make no gifts to them'

We are intangible creatures
separated

from the world
by layers

of light.

*

Each body a curve
   or curse, to rend the
days' cursive
       obliterated unity...

'or pat my instep to gain . . . [any favor] . .'

       Waking oneself in mid-
   passage, the dates and employment
           nameless, errands

separate, coeval...we are taking
walks
       without god.

   *

Waking early, sometimes
noting the sounds of birds

close to 5 a.m. A record
of movement, the complacency

of waking
that is itself ritualized.

   *

And if we took our heart
out, here, inside

the room that is less
mournful when you

return—

Fold your body
into mine

for comfort
& solace...

*

As yesterday sitting in the train car pulling
out of Lansdale the train stopped between
stations.... I noted the fields had
yellowed, each tree lining the road
blackened from a late rain, as a few
pink bands appeared in the evening sky.

'Trees I am familiar with here....'
Oak & cedar. Linden & Tulip.
Elm, fir & maple.

A line of blackened elms bordering the fields
as we passed.

*

I drifted apart from you   language
survivor   as one keeps

notes on the table
to resurrect

the form of another
reduce the

body to these turns
of phrase

Over the doorway
a signature key

blessed by your passing.

*

One night in the 80's
on Atlantic Avenue

I saw a gull descend
from the sky

its bright
wings

lit by street lamps

'I stopt to look…you
may if you choose

stop and imagine…'

Each of us completes a sentence
like pantomime passed through

a closing door.

*

Waking to 'catch a sign…

      tired along the shores of Brooklyn
as any oftener, no doubt, it flies by me
          as unknown as my neighbor's
dreams.—'

joined by what is a thread
at most of piecemeal

rendering. 'Your life
at once unremarkable

& absolved of its
declarations.'

This single route among many….

*

Unnatural to the last
day   the dead can't

speak otherwise

Bright track of rain

setting over the Brooklyn
waterfront   silver

on a black screen.

I'm staring into the last
portrait of a man

dead now more than
130 years.

*

Notebooks are lighter
put in one's pocket

the hills of another
era
            semblances
of perfect thought

'A pure sky, the
temperature just right.'

Co-equal beings
at sunset.

*

Blue theorem—

      as each day
is provenance, a spirit of
           delay—

We aren't sure but the sameness
can become a form of witness, no less
real than any 'poem incarnating
the mind of an old man'

Each person is like the other
        inside its habitat, what will be
    offered, here, what will be revealed
           as new work...

*

      Wandering away at
night, not listening, but craving
company in the Presbyterian
cemetery, stones dating back
to the early 1800's. I pull a rock
off one grave, left there by
family or friends, turned soft
in my hands.

*

Not morning but a sense
of its drift,
           so like water, the river
      can't sustain its surface
                any longer than wind
         cuts the body
                     from its moorings.

*

      Surrogate clothing, skin
color deepens, purple & blue, ply by ply
           one comes to read
      the grave sites anew, cyclamen
           at the edges of vision

Naked as we once were but
enfolded in this
                Joy Joy Joy

Soft coats and vests
the cotton lining
           worn thin, we are living
here long enough to breathe

this costume out.

*

'It's in his walk…the carriage of his
neck…the flex of his waist and knees'

And the hunters
haul up close
        with their unwilling
    horse, and taunt and curse
  away from dim light

an evacuant spilled
out of Heaven.

*

    You linger where it's safe to say the
years, so soft, have blackened along your
  left thigh…

the back of one's
neck, like a flower

crushed & separated.

*

Skin and grass, Pipe cleaners laid end to
end on a desk in sunlight. I am curious
to note the objects as a set, then freed
from any set. One by one my fingers
go across each object....

*

As the natural and perfect
slowly return from the
fire—

The plurality of voicing
that is essential to the
process

—'I grow I do not lag—I do not hasten—'

I didn't spend the days
yesterday or any other, but stayed behind

traversing these imaginary lines
of congress.

*

'As I look over the field, these yellow
wings everywhere mildly sparkling, many snowy
blossoms of the wild carrot gracefully bending
on their tall and taper stems—while for sounds,
the distant guttural screech of a flock of guinea
hens comes shrilly yet somehow musically to
my ears.' —August 4, 1878

The patterns of one
temporality that bleeds

into another. Watering
the garden at sundown

loose green fencing
positioned to ward off

strangers. An idle set of
facts recurring, breathed in

for comfort's sake.
I am their parent

relocated by the hour.

*

Lines of light, the
        opening rift—so it comes
to inhabit my own time   this hour among
billions—

   the road   low-lying trees   garden

at sunset.

Each one waking
on earth

without sign
of God.

A rose blackening in early
    October
        Saturn and Capella

Arcturus slowly descending
           to the west...

II

At night the moon
travels, the gods stay awake...

The Epic of Gilgamesh (tr. Sophus Helle)

And his skin was bright
gold in the locust season, his eyes
when he saw another
turned away...

So one can wander, reverse
course, shield this sheltered space
filled with light that
forms common days, threads one's
life together...

What I'm after....low pitched
    pools of southern
light, singly the season parts company
with the one before it, a yearly
shadowing, locust frost, I take my
 father's cane in hand, sweet rye, a settlement
in mind, how many were we
first here—

    At passing's variance, pitch, cool
loam, the sky wet, hard to the touch, barely
perceptible, as polity is a bridge, unaccountable
  at the back of a parking lot, the April
light, how it moves backward &
    forward across the grey backs
of vehicles....I'm carrying their
  cargo, the singleness of any one

    at this hour before dawn, to wait
for their movement into April, a sweetness
to what we see, the air, lotus-light
    was it seven to seven, the earned
income from these bridges, past
recall, wet, southern rail, to bridge these
beams...

Through how many seasons inspect
death's impact on locality, earth
fascicles, glued together
as Dickinson brought her
letters into the light, seasonal
   'and there was a smell of mint
under the tent flaps'
                    Amherst
light mixed with the sweetness of Pisa, one is
alighting here & there, among these cubits
of chance, one remembers little
where it was, a bird held up
   bedecked by light—

Spring language, settling
here, to rake the leaves out of
gutters, blue bulbs, near the
brickwork, a line of
       jonquils, green as rain.

   *

  As any days is decisive
as the next, as Dickinson wrote
Higginson February 10-13, 1876:

     'You asked me if I liked
the cold—but it is warm now. A mellow
Rain is falling.'

   *

My mother's purse opened to reveal
a few dollars, lipstick, the remnants
of a candy bar

stuck to the linen lining.

*

Yet the dreams are penitential, refutative
as if one closed a door on Self. I

woke from the 3rd, the 4th, the 5th
variations, in each one the light was

pellucid rimmed by smoke, a channel
of tobacco, the arc of one lifetime

melded to another's. I had your
skirts newly pressed, the visitation

of a son by his mother. Early the
following day, the 6th dream

in which you followed me into the
garden, lay down in the peony bed

a thousand years you said another
thousand can't fill this space.

*

Even as each return
promises another
    becoming.
I was dreaming of Apsu—
    blue earth, semi-oval
cape of dung, the sweet extension
    of floral covering, naked
as any limb is decked
            with leaves—

to cut through their mesh
inside the waters
    that receive, recede, as one
must renew participation—
    daily reveal where dying
is local, simplify the branch
    that falls across the front
of our house, so little
light, one navigates the earth
    at variance, schooled in what
is birth-given, notational
            veined cloth, paradigm
    of Gaia's gift.

*

                    Laid over
our single house the red
sky—
                    western hills
slow to change, movement's
hillside, a reliquary, eastern plot line
suburban sovereign, singly the emptying
out of space, yoked by these
rivers—Ohio & Chesapeake —dawn's literal
    transom, blue grey
                    falcon, polarized
                            aloft—

Salvaged for the last days
without temper or
realism

        'prayers for the dying
at yard's end' Whitman may have
laid his hands over how
many in paradise, their eyes not so
different, here inside the
eastern light, cloth hanging from a
storm drain, and south of
this landing, another's
    journey, hinterland, shaded
by stained lamp posts, blue 'shores
    of water, the path by the swamp
                in the dimness...'

*

One must be patient, you said, the hours
reward patience. I had learned to speak
your language, awkwardly, without skill
yet a form of talk emerged. At night
what did I say that caught you off-
guard. White peonies in the hard
moon light.

*

Not wet, glowing
from inside one's shirt, house
to house, a memory plain
baked into the scene—

     'the ice cream treat at Carver /

     bring in description of hospitals toward last / '

I'm returned to a day
in spring—clothed—bright
line, to gauge each
   dent in ground cover, erratic
spacing, seeds thrown here into
ragged cover, blue anemone, corded
      cape of sweet jonquil—
pale, as yet unseen.
   No recognition—here in
earth's night, seventeen days later
the sound of others moving
outside.

*

A gift of disclosure, to be sure
the realism of
grown men
he said, grown to live
out their time, here atop
mounded
spring earth—

     'The first wounded, came in a
     curious manner, on foot, hobbling, stragglers &c'

at break of day
east of their encampment
     hard light
  sun-up not recorded
by any visitant.

*

Yet the road
you eye is this

simple plane
between two

objects in a
low falling

sun. One's
body bends

over to
receive its

objects.

*

To draw back   winter
nearer than before   one keeps
          house to oneself
a record of keeping to
oneself—'I have these eyes
to give you'—intricate
late thought that hides itself
   here, ghostly movement through
this landscape. Keep it to yourself
says it one time, then the renewal of
waiting—a kind of gift to keep
to oneself—'the poem wants to go
in'—a permanent record of doing
so, again and again—

          where yesterday the white
blooms—apple blossoms—appeared
mnemonic—against a screen on the train
returning from Lansdale—this cusp
of reunion—black sycamores—
christened by the roadside…

*

The incidents too
numerous to count. Ribbed

loss, western
star....Each is a compass

of 'mourn and ever-
returning spring.'

Temporality's
wandering eye, my

cross-eye that waits
its turn, noting 'a sprig

with its flower'
as if shape and color

were of one form.

The grief sustaining
& perpetual.

Sweet sane deaths...

*

Though the hours come back
as ordinary, you tell them by

how often the figures disappear.

Once inside the dreamscape
I saw a friend from childhood

walking into the yard next to
ours. His face brightened as

he leaned into the saw-sound
from tree men come to cut

down the overhanging
branches of oaks and elms.

I lay next to the window a
long time watching him

remain outside, the low
autumn light separating

each branch as it fell.

*

The books are weighted
by water as Dickinson

prophesied, you can take
them through the orchard

above Hadley, MA near a field
where a young man once took

his life. It's said he didn't
intend to go, thought it would

be a slow drop, then
weightlessness. His arms

when they found him
pinned to his sides

his head tilted upward.

*

Inside & out, the newly
won daylight. 'Now the grass

tomorrow the stiff curl
of wildcarrot leaf'

Williams in 1923, too
early to see rays of sun

past river and dry land, here in the
east where Ohio is west, the long

yield of color, aptly
named 'june light' for it

cancels out spring, keeps
days separate, as red light

smooths the onion patch
near where children

came to play, circular
games of hide & seek

parallel to field poppies.

*

Or your eyes—

to simplify the radiance, not
effort but a gain in time, the real

loss is spare, cool to the
touch, as Niedecker understood

at flood tide when things
are consumed by water.

*

The opening flowers
pressed against one's flesh...

ribbons of pale spring
light, gives way, godless

to less & less of oneself
where Ea floods the ground

and Enlil narrows his eye
toward the parting

hawk...

*

The days come & go. A fifth
night, a sixth, a seventh, an eighth

without dreaming of anything
or anyone. A fifth night, a sixth.

I lay near the window without
covers, my body turned toward

a low-hanging moon.

*

'Pictures of growing
spring and farms and homes...'

Every simple idea
carries one idea from its source—

realism separate from what
gave it life, as I re-enter the park

near the harbor, evenings so quiet
along Baltimore's streets

moving out of Fells Point
the only enjoyment

river scent drawn from
the harbor at night.

What begins as story
ends in image, a carryover

from childhood when I
passed the days staring into the

trees above our house, watching
each branch catch the light

then let go.

*

As if walking against the tide
to enter his room again—

at peace my father said he'd been
visited seven times by an angel

on earth he said as in heaven
the waters would claim us

later the sun broke through
and he said it was a form of salvation

practiced by the faithful.

*

     The lateness of the hour is common
among our dead. Waiting on the seventh step
toward my room upstairs—

     I am given to understand my place
inside the transcription. A healing remonstrance.
A weight of silver & copper. Your head

neither hard nor cold but pressed into sweet
marjoram leaves. 'I believe the earth is meant
to offer us back,' here on earth the offer

is twofold: like a bird coated in grey feathers—
not seeing light but the bird's weightlessness
as it leaves the earth.

*

As Whitman made a list
of gods, the pages yellowed

you can hear their names
spelled out—

Phtah Isis Osiris   Kronos

To render their titles
on boards that float

into the water
yellow bands of light

systemically enfolding
each letter.

*

Wind returns
not light but absence of care

Zephry's breeze
last seen in measures of water.

Hands adjust one's
clothing, to enter

these spaces, anew
crossing through

eras as if each
had spooled thread

into our hands.

What is recognized
as long gone, settled

the understanding
that reverberates

inside a clustered plastic
shell.

*

If I hand myself over
will you catch me?

Earth's solitary plover.
A ring of Saturn. You

pronounce my name
again so I can hear it in

two then three languages.
Earth cloth woven from each

triangle of silk. You are
bearing the intimacy

of creation, as a songbird
whitens in a yard next to mine.

*

I have been gone 36 days
and nights, now come home

to see things shifted out of position.
Stones moved by rain

from their place on the path.
Garden pots disturbed by rabbits

and squirrels. The myrtle branches
to the west of our upper windows

bent from a hard wind.

And darkening like a route
through each day, the fields browning

in late August, 'the corn, stack'd in its
cone-shaped stacks, russet color'd

and sere.'

*

As course is cut, Osiris
winters here

so lingering Ra

the lattice
broken

windows ashen
beneath a southern sky.

I can't repeat what I've done.
Here are hermitage and scale,

small covered bark pieces
elms at a slant

light shows them drenched
by rain again.

*

I had been reading of the return
of Ea, the longitudinal waters

crossed, as pyres were set, the wind
that brokered their travels.

Was there one
in the company of two

a facility of trickster
heaven, soothsayer night

locality's angelic drift.

Wandering here, among these
low coasts of moon and Pennsylvania

corn, the whiteness
of each residence moved as if

the eye were a compass
turning north and south

and back again.

*

From one the other
the image of

one ring, of settlement
& its erasure. 'What

he commands he
doesn't erase, what

he sets down he
doesn't erase.'

Enkidu's voice set here
as marker and warning.

*

Water & the fruits of one's labor.
A strawberry field turned to mud after heavy rains.

*

Being double we can
part company with you.

A ridge, flight of the
falcon at dawn

one is dangling inside the
rift of heavenly light

preparing to read our way
back into the textuality

of birds, their realism
that affronts each river.

Po smooth as
a lake of mind.

One can't remember the parting
but winter was ploughed under again

unwound
by what greeted rocks underneath

in the light that is the light
of virtu as Pound understood it.

Sunt lumina, a particular smell advancing
our body tensile and rapt

as if to become present here
were to re-invent each rhapsode's cycle.

The practice that was present
in Yao, the precision in Shun

admired from this distance.
Yearly compassions of water, wind

yellowed bands of
jonquils

a spring that is not yet here.

*

The reading provides
continuity....

Abjection as *obsidian, carnelian, lapis lazuli...*

As if to enter their
community were to re-write

one's place among
the historic dead. I revised

each day, turned lotus
wing to dust, read

until dawn to see its light skillfully
re-worked. The Soul

moves across & into
each blade, carrying with it

a book of days.

*

Here, at pond's edge, the loon
I'm hearing, skillful, paratactic, localized

by light that gleams out of its shell.

So much is practice, the yearning to re-enter
skin, whose prayers Ea recites

the prayers of one's life
resumed, brokered by gloire

as if outside oneself
existed the resumption of glory

like wild birds
encountered in a night vision

here and away, the emptying
out of sky, these uneaten portions

of bread and seed
thrown into water.

*

Years ago Olson sitting in his room
in Washington D.C. could hear the

capital at night, inside the ring of
its light, his time there, 'birds

upon the earth,' he was privy to
their logic, as if maintained by

seers, public sadness that was
its own counsel, as he reproduced

what was for Whitman longstanding
grief, a metallic taste in the mouth.

*

What steadies
                 the days, looser gait at the hillside's break.
        Water loosened from inside
                 a human skull. Pieces of ribbon.

The ageless bird that Olson traced on blank sheets.

Each part of America
    'we speak with water...on our
              tongues'
        as if to put earth's rivers back inside us.

Come near its waters, blue
              Potomac, and drink
        with our tongues newly minted.

What can be imagined
can be undone in a lifetime.

Here inside a channel of Potomac
    we endure Ea's whisper across America
        at one with what's returned
              spoken & re-spoken, no drum

but this skin cut from tent fabric.

        *

'Now you can come back,' one
is saying from another room.

I read back the day's ledger, a foil
for my 'self,' here in the gleam of shell

light I go to speak with water, stranded birds
caught in a triptych of sound

an ambient of change, sequestered
Potomac signals. We fall onto

its shores again, ready to remove
ourselves from earth's 'yellow gold

sinking sun...homeward returning.'

*

And balanced between states—
arrival is skin time. Balance of white
        lotus and peony. Flowers of memory
                spring. A fraught light. So many

        moved by what's been removed. To unseat
light when the new season begins. Ghostly
                prematurity. Wet to the tongue.

        Eyes erase what they took in. Flowers
shaved from the ground, a signal of black leafy
                vines, sharpen and wake the body.

        The way one
wakens now is not the same as yesterday.
        Or the day before that. A sort of stick-figure
                says our name, recollection's cell opened
        again…

        There is morning, thick light….Combed over
                rows of Saturn light. The dawn Hesiod says
        claims only one third a portion of our day's work.

        Dawn gives a head start. River light as the
season opens out. Cumberland County is east of here.
                I am mapping the congress of vines to ply
        their names on earth.

        Our arms
                lifted in folds of shadow from the west.

\

In blue heavens a flight of geese forms a 'v' then re-
      shapes into a scythe, pulled from each side
            through layers of early evening light.

      Systems pour out their diagrams. I have one
companion to come, hidden behind a crepe myrtle, the utterances
          of strangers in the parking lot…far from this
      post, another is waking, sitting down

      to steer his prayers. River goats travel
in a line I am pursuing to the west. One animal
         at a time, I am moving as a dog star

       moves, one day after the other, hoeing the
            field in late summer, one day

        after another, hawk
           and lair of light, held up to the sun
early dusk & mid-August's goat milk
              & meat from a free-roving heifer…

      In the dusk one day after
the hawk has flown over, a change to wind patterns
        signals an early crossing. My plot unchecked

       flows east to west
         and back again….

chickadee — large brown water=dog —
— black=snake — garter snake —
— vinegar=plums — persimmon —
— ~~oto~~ white=blossomed dog=wood —
— sweet potato — plum=trees —
 plum orchard
— cedar — chestnut —

The suicide ~~that hanged herself~~
          went to a lonesome place
          with a pistol and killed
          himself, ~~and~~ I came that way and
                    stumbled upon him
_____
                    birch
locust, ~~birch with white and ringed~~
          cypress — buttonwood —
_____
          ~~large worm~~   reckon
~~O don't you beloved!~~ I ~~guess that~~ you are
~~I am the the~~ ~~corpse~~ — ~~I am the~~ good manure
— but that I do not smell. beautiful white
— I smell your
     roses — your leafy
I kiss ~~the your soft~~ lips — I ~~reach~~ slide my
     hands for the brown melons
     of your breasts. —

III

Any morning
return is hierarchical   blue
storm clouds   from the west
predictions of high winds
by nightfall…

What assures life its momentum
to pass the days inside
        rope walk leaning into its
sweet mint & thyme

parcels of weed
in cracks along the walk.

*

        In dear company
a yard is two days out
from the shelter
        of a tree lost to high wind

3 weeks ago

        light now enters this space
unimpeded   so that any

*

Yet any habitat—how long
having lived here, moving into
   the 3rd decade, wind
smooth from the east, a Gilbey's
gin bottle I carry from
      another lifetime.

*

How do I lift
color, smooth stain on
yellow flooring—open
to its singular
                  line—

As light settles into
   black trees, the years
   open against all
         instruction

*

'And who's dead and who isn't'

in this time, to watch
the calendar, motifs of this
   historical span, yielding
cyclical re-reading

movement both into
& out of
      harm's way.

*

If any moves
    into its ending---
And what's come
round, as station, black
    notes in hand, I'm
dreaming of this other

common time, adrift, so many
smells congregate in one
hall, house-blind
            or gone altogether
    from eyesight.

*

Midday I'm late to see the
light—all down the
signs, passed on, we're
    relatable to your days

 'small is my theme—
yet hast the sweep of the universe'

that comes as instruct
the dead reading
us back to ourselves
I said some time
back
            here the pattern
is no less pertinent

for having been
reallocated as wish.

*

As so many combine
generous to a fault, what can be
unthought, as prayer, loose
change on the ground
   of heaven, you can't
unbuy death. Unbury
its soundings…here on
   beggarly earth—

all skin is gestural
in place of found objects
the heart so scarce it comes
   to begin again, wind-
whipped child, any day
now, the woman at the window
passing on, her undrunk
   neat drink.

*

Not meeting
but in the doing
a decade Whitman
writes toward
the infinite—

back of him / of us

Rainwater on a Washington street
ca. 1862—

    Dante comes near
as the action of the poem
(Whitman notes) begins
  on Good Friday 1300

noting he was 35
when he began, 56
at time of his death.

      'To praise
paradise from afar is to
      come back as an angel—'

*

'We remember that first
of April at the post
office, when the young man
in the linen jacket   blotched with ink
handed through the window
a very rare envelope, promising great things,
we found nothing at all inside
but a piece of blank paper—'

Viewing from my window
tranquil stars
your body as signpost

to each parting figure.

*

The obligation to report
what's found.

Simple objects laid out for viewing.

Compass. Pen knife. Steel ring.

The economy of each
stenciled artifact. A diagram

from inside the man's left
coat jacket pocket.

'Can you come back tomorrow?'

A phrase more reticent
than belief.

*

You can withstand
anything, in time to repeat
it comes as charge, single
file, the schoolhouse
drill—

awake in any weather
our mother might have shaken us

back to our senses
'habit is mindless,' my mother
said, the routine a dull
glass, grey from
inside, whale
meat, corn on the
cob, thrown into the

trashcan. Nights are no
way to meet another.

*

What's any street but
a passing on of many
   you can say the load
is less abundant, the
gain hard to tell.

Ageless, as Pound saw it
so many hours to 10, a painted
river, the movement it
made—*terra nova*—why not
   rebuild with prayer
from the green room, this late

season of renewal.

*

'The Day came slow—'

to the bottom of an
orchard where the body
remained unfound
for six days

sundown to sunup
a gentle rain fell.

*

And mis-
   remembering
my father in July
not pain but
exaction, to his
benefit, the sky
   emptied of
birds, he

      came down
   a window pulled
      from inside his
   eyes—

as Whitman wrote of
another no less
proud man

'He stood at the door
   the first Sunday—
helped the sexton
show people to seats—proud
      of his building and wealth.'

      *

Parataxis in place of persons.

The days receive us—patronymic & matronymic—
scale and space.

Complacent light. A sweet
darkness enfolding

canopied lilies.

*

All day—
reaching back to these
   first hours here—

canopy, light's orange
tip, lattice-like
   to make rain from

pages of light
cinnamon, blue-
hinged flute…

> 'I am sitting on a remnant of a pine log, the old groundsite
> of what probably a large camp hut. I can see to the south-
> east of the depression in the landscape, where the Rappahannock
> runs, one or two signs of Fredericksburgh (a battery could easily
> shell it from where I sit).'

Sharing breakfast
with no one the frost

visible through the
dining room

window. Earth
tones. A small

line between grass
and walkway.

The birds in
docile rows.

I am nearer to You
than they are to me.

*

Doing the math
in one's head—for
oneself a day by day
    activity—

break bread here
with Whitman as debts
must be paid

Blue skies of 1st of June
in Pennsylvania the mourning
doves & robins
        early morning ritual

at this remove to read from underneath
a canopy of low lying
hills to the west

keeping company here
in these boundaries of
solitude
        re-composed

fable of recurring
relation.

*

And the chickadee
at sunrise & slow call
of the mourning dove—

how patiently we await
earth's turns

blue grey skies without rain.

IV

I saw no Way – The Heavens were stitched –
I felt the Columns close –
The Earth reversed her Hemispheres –
I touched the Universe –

Emily Dickinson (833, R.W. Franklin edition)

What can be observed—
cloth movement, single pole attached
to a moving wave—

Earth's hours are subjectless
as neither one nor
the other
can resolve

patterns—synecdochic
recovery, wave after
wave—

another morning of color
fastened to a broken sail—we say
'carved fleet of 50 sails'
meaning the month has passed
on water, sweet sevens dropped
into a sequence

of one.

*

I have no testimony but the earth
that moves, great beginnings
inside this lexicon
of images—

what was written there, inside the left
pocket of a man's waistcoat, not morning
but the aftermath of its
application, so that by four he made
a sequence of poverty, the lone
braid of hair, swept under the rug.

Here too it's eidolon, shape-shifter, after-the-
debt of all debts, to rend oneself
incoherent—what station was it I saw at 61
a bird moving slightly west of east—
skyline, pole, tipped with silver

like a foil for god.

*

And each house
is neither holy nor derelict—

common hands supplicate
along these posts
as any is a source of
comfort at day's
end—

What can I do but remember
your soul—effort
as movement into the clean
daylight
          out along the shores of Paumanok
where you were born, birth shine
so clean the leaves
skittle past—newly found

what can the hands invent
but portions of reality—

Unhoused as we once
may have been, the gambit
to take back each shell
from its cabinet
& lay it inside another's
breast pocket

o dreamt of shine
shaped like a lingual
scar—a four-leaf
disc of skin.

*

Marriage is an arrival—

meeting time, the spring flowers—draped
on patterned lawns—

sweet May—the ending is what
was cleansed by rainwater

inside a steel
pail.

*

Inside a steel
pail—the rain is less

what it says than
another form

of intuition
memory as lode

star, embankment, green
play station, to roam

habitual, as sky
norms us all, each

bathed in the
oak's shell, suited

to form inside
columnar shadows

as dress & limbs
move into each

other, break their
bonds as close-up the

agents of change
are nearer than one

ever thought.

*

'Here, lilac with a branch of pine,
here, out of my pocket some
                moss which I pull'd off a live-
oak in Florida as it hung
                trailing down'

So that each saturated day
smooth cataract of this & that
appearances that linger

west of each branching
tongue of light, this recurrent realism
of currants and wild orange

            'things, thoughts, the stately
            shows of the world,
            the suns and moons,
            the landscape, summer
            and winter,
            poems, endearments'

One is dead or alive
thrust back or forward
into these lairs of song.

*

Normative light.
One is interchangeable

with what one has removed
disk after disk, interchange

of serial affection. The branch
moved into place, above

a compos'd well, a bunch of
wild orange, the composition

now drawn from water, things &
thoughts of things

the stately show

of the world, suns and
moons, the landscape

of afternoons without
one body, but these manifold

spirits, attending, stems of
currents, twists of maple

a bunch of wild orange
and chestnut

                *

As any day is less than the spirit
of that day, the intricate thickness

spelled in groundwork, a bridge, the cathexis
beyond oneself. Here in longitudinal

space, errant, walking hurriedly backward
across Chestnut St., to lose the ability to recall

daylight, any seer in the west, the locality
of song, here in the divided space, which

half do you compose, which do you misdirect?

*

And what can be remembered—
half-thought
        the delay in receiving one's
        children, halfway through
   the day there is no time left
to see them—

Each in the separate
locality of another's time frame.

If we inhabit one moment
without prejudice, the clarity
'perched among words'
   as if to inhabit one space
without language—

these figures of speech
proposing a belief

in god.

*

Gift packet, space inside
the Ohio dream of
       salt, rain, sweet
        seed light that is its own accompaniment.

Reading in a dream
state, the language both foreign
& slipped from consciousness
    as so many vowels
may be slipped into the hands
       of a stranger—

'visitation's earnest companion'
blue
      at the edge of one river.

*

The biography of stillness
is read back to us daily. Your sojourning

here a kind of companionship
without end. To retrace

the crow's flight. Sky lines.
Itinerant visitant venturing

across the landscape.

*

I had been wakened
by your image—
        first its nakedness
    a pool of evergreen shade
low sweet embers of
        my father's casket. I'd
    taken soft weed, spilled

melded rosemary with
thyme, the bluest
        shade of water
    refracting your headless
torso, so it can become
        enshrined, despoiled
    & new again.

*

Somehow to redirect
energy, a project given over to
time, these root
        scenes—

pocketbook, black note
tucked into the leaf
        all change is mercurial

blue ring of flame
inside one's back pocket.

*

I was this stranger, not yet
anyone's, but here & again

the elemental year, a fort-
night, blue-black

across the roofs of D.C.
where the crows kept

still, so the daylight weakens
over Potomac, how the

day undresses the body
as song melts, not iterative

but prolonged gaiety, as
change moves through

epigraphic stillness.

*

      'Of seeds, dropping into the
ground, of births,
         of the steady concentration
            of America'

as 'not even now – so sweet'
the elements of our nature

persist unsaid.

*

Not one but several
days, the ground
          blackened, steadied
by poplar and chestnut—

tiled roofs at a distance
longitudinal grace
          of one hour among
these people—
                    hovering, balanced
     above ground, the pooled
          phatic string—

pulled through blooms
of perpetual summer.

          *

As the property lights
come on the same time

each evening around
5 p.m. casting a line

of shadow across
each grass lot. I lean

toward them, then
pull my body out of view

beneath windows
facing southwest.

A tree in the distance
as rooftops recede.

Slowly the shapes recur.

A system of inner color
I call my own. Here in evening

light & its patterns
no nearer to you

than I.

*

Empathy

for what can't be seen.

Black screen door

opens in the distance. A child

upstairs with the window open.

Unhoused sky, 'the audiblest

at dusk,' each in its person

separated by what enjoins them.

*

But the spirits

    effusing mind

    & character—

No winter or sign

of threat, the water

closer at day's end

you can follow the edges

of river, Potomac darker

to the touch, as one moves

out to gather

    dried leaves

& cut blossoms.

The arousal

is sempiternal, water

looser to the touch

than a mouth of dried

grass, for these are spirits

    come from afar.

*

'No man and no woman can

starve or overburden

or imbibe stuff in

    his or hers, any more than one

    can poison or starve his body.—'

To remember is to re-locate

one's other self, belonging

here, at the river's

    blue edge, night

bearing wind, Chesapeake

night, slow-moving

    falls in the

    click of a moment.

*

And each is a politics
of becoming, the yearning
completes itself
         as window yarn, plastic
     awning, pulled down
                 to ground-level

where irises show their
colors, deepened
         by moonless light.

*

These lessons of inherency
as repeated grafts

limb for limb. Trees
outside one's vision

populate the space regardless.
The acquisition of sight

again & again offering
potential objects outside

oneself. Limbs loosened
by winter. Bare signs

of perennial growth.

*

What continues is the rhetoric
of astonishment. Elbow to
        elbow, nothing doing
    but candle time, sweet hanging
lift O the shine they make
        so low to the ground, one is
            astonished to find
    the body so limber at this
                age, it can wash
    itself clean, renewed together.

But common days are not
easy, the weight
    shed, the task
political, for a depth
    of light, here in the
poplar stream where I
    am waiting, a reader
of signs, de Certeau tells
            us, days are thinner
    when you ascend, a circle

like loops of ice
water, straddling the form
    of every woman & man
braids of nautical time
            that hold each unit
separate, each body
        adrift among its
                companions.

*

And when I am here
I am also there—the not-yet-
there you said was part
of the dance, to re-create
where one has been, forest
among the trees, as though
lingering in these last
hours you could find a
home here, inside the honored
gods, bone-dead, so one is
after all a repository of
so many to come, & each
raises the color to name
a kingfisher's gait, offered
as recompense, dark
companions of the forest
ablaze with public names.

So that the archive is always
ablaze—

And each of us moving toward it....

*

The corrective memory
latent, yet progressive
through how many
      altered states
  the fingers are picking
up signs, simple to
      translate, word
games in one's old mind
        to gather the dead
    is no new trick, ease

of one's skill, dry leaves
on a porch, the wind
        carries them off.

   *

Winter sun not yet
a fallen thing, the predictions
notwithstanding
          each day is consumed
     by what it gave back
        an edginess to our
inquiry—

no one can stay still
for very long, migrant
love is empeopled
at this remove

          Our love is still
less than what was promised—
duration's kept secret
open to inspection.

                    'I think a few my right hand is time
                    and my left hand is space—both are ample—
                    a few quintillions of cycles, a few sextillions
                    of cubic leagues, are not of special importance to me—'

The grooves of our
holding still, in place, as if
to return were the same
as to depart...

And what is matter returns
as phenomena, the ordinariness
of any day that completes
a turn

        left to chance the rain
        resumes without notice

        hills go dark from lack of such

        what is witnessed thereby removed
        from comprehension.

℔ — This is the Earths word —
the pervading sentiment or lesson is to
be that the only good of learning
the theory of the ~~largeness, &c~~ fluency, and generosity
and impartiality, largeness and
exactitude of the earth is to
use all those toward Character — human
Character

As thought is
bound by what it can't
  retrace—this joyousness
of song—

Or respite, as wind from the
northeast blasts through, no paper
or wire to hang the day
  through & thru

these relics of repair, sorted out
journal by journal, one
waits at the end
        to find some laces, small
tins of shoe black—

the rims of these
objects, possibly re-gathered
                for fall.

*

And if I remember
the darkness of Ohio, can I

retrace its timbre, steel
light from the west, a hill

I sat near, house to the south
of my left side, the ring

of cloth, carried from inside
my room, bluer than teal

larkspur rising
from inside a green

margin...

*

    'Poem incarnating the mind of an old man, whose life
    has been magnificently developed—the wildest and
most exuberant joy—'

Yet reimagined as
god, partially obscured
at sky light's
    partition, the clean
blue line, tented

to keep the dead at bay.

*

I have no reference
beyond what I

can reproduce in
washed linen, black

& tan ribbed
blouse, the unhoused

patience of my
mother, Iris, bending

into the daylight—

Wash day she is hanging
wet clothes on the line

close to her left eye
a single lick of eye shadow

pegs in her hands
put space back into light.

*

As any light
is this one   pushed aside
a seal   black bobbin

spun from one's   dear
left hand   the rest   apart

from daylight   October or November
light   the simple mirror I'm carrying

jewel thief   born to mend
this fence   not another   of one

minute, cracked open   quicksilver
Thoreau called it   will never wear

off   our hands scrubbed
bloody in Potomac's   ebbing

tide.

*

The slowest remedy
written back as soil.

Carbon water.
A hole inside the sky

where daylight was.
Perennial growth of late blooming flowers.

Embarrassed by their color
I turn away, freed to re-name

them as I wish.

*

'a fish can leap or an insect fall'   but in each

circle   the fish or insect   insists
on a line of clarity   a restless plurality

of song   'gentle pulsings of this
life….'   leaf and twig and stone

handed back thru   a spring morning
no weather set   nothing so fair or simple

as these objects   bluer than
ice   'its surface ever fresh'

*

And what I hold
a barren track you walked

out of view the sky
gently descending

like prophecy
from inside

each drought-stricken limb

as rain comes the first time
in 61 days

to dampen the ground

encamped here
as we are.

*

And west of here
waters of Ohio flowing

back across a landscape
I'm interpreting

from memory.
Each change charted

from within. I kept
vigil with these lines

at variance from what
I wrote the day before.

Language loss
as a temporary state.

The nouns failing
us, the mind seeks other

branches. Windows
open to a light wind.

The indirect as much
as the direct. The Soul

I keep is the Soul I
sought.

*

Ordinary days. Blue
light, a ribbon of salt

lining the walk. One
sparrow alighting

on its feeder. Numinous
days in which to inhabit these

visions of company.
Kindred spirits

returning with us.

9 October 2022-30 November 2024

CODA:
ON THE POETICS OF INTERMEDIACY

Lovely, the Dreams and Chance Encounters
but Now   is wedded thruout to   the Intention of a Universe.
Robert Duncan, "Passages: Jamais"

This book is a continuation of a number of books I've written across the last several years that have devoted themselves to the form of the daybook. Serially written, *The Fire Cycle* and *Daybooks: North & East* documented or sought to document noticings, the quotidian, the small terms of daily life. A practice I sometimes carried out daily, extending into months or ceasing after several days, to be picked up again, as repetition and recursiveness became the governing processes of these books. At the same time, both earlier books took as core principles the states of otherness in the "I" writing and experiencing the pull of the temporal at a distance from any root formation of self. Immersion and resurfacing could be key metaphors for the experiences written into these books, as I worked with Du Fu, Pound, H.D., Basho—companions enroute with me in a journey without clear origin or endpoint. Insofar as presentness was key, so too was disarrangement and non-linearity, as if to settle in one place of haptic relation required an intermedial space before and after, relying on a requisite incompleteness that the serial form demanded of the poems. Often without clear presence in a relational "present," the poems that accumulated could appear dislodged from time, separated from social and public life in a meditative sideshadowing of the real.

Invoking Mnemosyne, the Greek goddess of memory, the poem that is *Whitman at the Bardo* worries—is troubled through and by—the intermedial site of death-in-life, of life that has not yet moved into death but exists as claimant and petitioner, shadow and light. As we read in *Tibetan Book of the Dead*:

Alas, now as the intermediate state of the time of death arises before me,
Renouncing all attachment, yearning and subjective apprehension in every
        respect,
I must undistractedly enter the path, one which the oral teachings are clearly
        understood,
And eject my own awareness into the uncreated expanse of space.
Immediately upon separation from this compounded body of flesh and blood,
I must know this body to be like a transient illusion.

Translated by Gyurme Dorje

We renounce attachment while holding to a Subject we understand as embodied, lived-through and with. Memory is conditional and provisional here, insofar as it relates the self to an ongoing past that blurs our sense of temporal emplacement. We are here, not here, elsewhere, moving through and away from the signposts of daily existence. Our body becomes both the proving ground of self and its sequential re-enactment, at the same time it is in the separation between "this was" and "this will be" that we find temporality itself dislodged, turned away from us. It's in this flux that we experience reflexive time that is neither inside nor outside but irrecoverable chronology. A kind of codicil to our awareness of language as enactment and estrangement, the plurality of movements at any instant that define and elude understanding. In his *Blue Book*, Ludwig Wittgenstein describes the movement of his hand and what it means to say one has lifted one's hand and touched one's eye or if the sentence can ever capture that process of distilled movement. A grammar of propositions. "My finger moves from my tooth to my eye." The "I" disappears, as an "Other" is made visible.

The long poem that is *Whitman at the Bardo* documents these traces of self. My own and/or another's. The seriality of days, as one + one + one moves the Self toward another position, another branch of possible fulfillment and enlightenment. The give and take of language that is ritualized, a flow of sentences one into the next seemingly without end. The day stops yet the language remains moving without us. The work is material and elusive at once, paratactic and hypotactic. A string of river stones hung across a nail.

*

How they sweep down and out! how they mutter! ^Poets^ unnamed — artists greatest of any ^with all their lost designs^, ~~Pride of manhood—tones of the dying~~ ^Love unre-^ ^turned—^ ~~age's complaints—hope's last words,Some suicide's despair~~^ing^ ~~cry, Away~~ ~~to the boundless waste, and never again return.~~
Transcription of Whitman's "Last of ebb and daylight waning," notebook entry, ca. 1885

I wrote the first drafts of this series in six separate writing sessions from October 9 to November 30, 2022. The impetus for the poem developed from a series of social media postings by Joseph Donahue in which he shared notebook images from the Walt Whitman digital archive. These notebook pages that appear as facsimiles of Whitman's poem drafts and notebooks served as a mediumistic set of prompts to the writing that would emerge across the next several weeks. Writing through these notebook pages, I came to understand this project as in part a formal and exegetical one, as I sought through transcriptions of Whitman, repetitions of phrasing and the re-presentation of language on the page. As with an earlier project of mine, *Drafts for Shelley*, I became transfixed with the fluidic movement of handwritten letters, the intermedial and out-of-time space these documents occupy, so that to read this Whitman moved me into the intermediacy of form and sign. The written and the unreadable. What is crossed out becomes read as a branch of alternative meaning, of the unsettlement of language on the page. To revisit these scenes of writing was to bring forward memories of my sitting in an airless classroom at John Eaton Public School in Washington, D.C. in 1st or 2nd grade and being required to practice handwriting in cursive using the Palmer method current at the time The pages of my marbled black and white composition book filled up with curved lettering that would become jagged at the tops and bottoms of letters, forcing me to re-draw them over and over again until my teacher finally relented and let me put aside the work for the day. It's a practice that became ingrained in my sense of what it meant to write by hand, to labor the way we can with pen or pencil and paper, even as my hand would develop across the years a form of writing that became more and more illegible, as if to write by hand were a form of self-silencing and censure.

*

The autobiographical strands of this poem—the reappearance throughout of my long-dead mother, Iris Mossin (nee Alford), who died by suicide at 51 in 1971, and my father, Richard Mossin, who died in 2003; the geographies of Washington, D.C. where I grew up; northeastern Ohio where I attended Wooster College for a year; the Pioneer Valley in Massachusetts where I would complete my undergraduate studies at Hampshire College; and the Potomac River that appears across the pages of this book—emerge through this work as recursive and blended narratives of by and large undated time. I move among these figures and landscapes as conditions of perpetual reenactment and renegotiation. Years apart from these people and the spaces they once occupied, I returned with Whitman in mind to revisit, relearn the language spoken between the dead and myself. "Collecting, dispensing, singing, there I wander with them."

"A really perfect poem has an infinitely small vocabulary," Jack Spicer famously wrote. I have sought to negotiate and meet the terms of that smallness throughout this book, that vocabulary, in serial progression that lingers inside each cursive movement, a scale of grammar learned early in life from the diagramming of sentences. To recognize meaning in any sentence was to behold its simplest formation as a line separated by other lines, dangling down, held in motion the way a rag unfurls on a line in mid-summer, the sun bleaching it dry again.

To see the world, one must know its objects and what moves them. Nouns and verbs. The actionable space of lingual performativity in the movement of a sentence to discover the vocabulary absent from oneself. "I couldn't remember the word for it," we say. "Give me a moment, it's coming to me." That lag—that stutter—marks the world of this poem that move formally between couplet arrangements and open form, shifting across registers to find the missing word(s). Cognitive delay as a form of contemplation and replenishment. The poem as word room, each stanza filled up, emptied out, as Whitman toward the end of his life saw his vocabulary return to him less frequently yet accountable and forceful when it did. "Good-Bye my fancy...."

*

"I did what I knew before I knew what I did," Olson once wrote. It's a statement that has stayed with me ever since I first encountered it many years ago while doing work for my book chapter on Olson and the correspondence with Frances Boldereff and Robert Creeley. Where Olson's reception still relies primarily on his daunting formal explorations and inquiries into the complex knit of politics and social identity dominant in *The Maximus Poems*, I returned to his work during the writing of this book to re-see the formal elements of poetry that I'd once absorbed and learned from. Here too were the ventriloquized and mimetic branches into sites of poetic statement and formal inquiry. The embodiment of language is its difficulty, as any of us is persistent and present in multiple languages at once. The leave-taking of one tongue is the formative site of another's telling, another's presence in the grammar of always changing self. This is to say: I know this work as composed of myself and of many others, a polyvocality that is at once solitary and public, an internment in the situated realisms of this poem.

Ascension has a muffled Route.

    E. Dickinson (Letter to Mary and Eben Jenks Loomis, early November 1884)

Daily habit provides the core of introspection. I go out and come back as one does over time at regular intervals, marked by traveling to work and returning home, housekeeping and rest. The low light at 4:30 in November that shifts to paler shades of blue green by April....For over a decade I've traveled by SEPTA Regional Rail between my home in Doylestown, PA and Temple University in Philadelphia, where I teach. The commute takes about one and a half hours, as I ride south through Chalfont, New Britain, Fortuna, Lansdale, and further south through Melrose Park, Jenkintown, and Fern Rock to end for me at Temple. Between Chalfont and Link Belt stations, our train usually stops to wait for the southbound (or northbound, depending on the direction) train to pass us at the start of a long stretch of single tracking to the end of the line in Doylestown. The stop can sometimes take up to 15 minutes, and each day as we sit unmoving on the tracks, I look west across a field I've been staring into since I first started riding the train to work in 2013. It is an unvaried yet deeply changing landscape, depending on the season. The sycamore trees along road that runs parallel to the train tracks lose and gain their leaves, hold color or disappear within a frame that includes sunrise and sunset. The emptied greenness of a field that once may have grown corn or soy but now sits fallow season after season, dirt yellow or brown, dry from drought or visibly saturated from a recent rain. It is quiet time I keep inside the train, often sitting in a mostly empty car among a few others, as I stare out across the fields and wait for the train to move forward again.

*

Recently, while working on this book, I came across this language from Whitman's *Specimen Days* after he'd moved to the New Jersey countryside outside of

Camden in the 1870s:

Lights and shades and rare effects on tree-foliage and grass—transparent greens, grays, & c., all in sunset pomp and dazzle. The clear beans are now thrown in many new places, on the quilted, seam'd, broze-drab, lower tree trunks, shadow'd except at this hour—now flooding their young and old columnar ruggedness with strong light, unfolding to my sense new amazing features of silent, shaggy charm, with many a bulge and gnarl uncheck'd before. In the revealings of such light, such exceptional hour, such mood, one does not wonder at the old story fables (indeed, why fables?) of people falling into love-sickness with trees, siez'd ecstatic with the mystic realism of the resistless silent strength in them—strength, which after all is perhaps the last completest, highest beauty.

I have followed Whitman's "mystic realism" in this book as he has opened the way for us to do so. The light that shifts across the Camden countryside falls again across the field in between Chalfont and Link Belt stations that I stare at. Our expression is both social and solitary, aleatory and realized daily as a practice of faith, an estrangement from and belonging to all that we've kept to ourselves throughout these conversations that move, silently, across such lines of open prose given back to us as poetry.

Doylestown, PA
18 December 2024

Notes & Acknowledgments

The photo representations of Whitman's notebook drafts are from *The Walt Whitman Archive*, Matt Cohen, Ed Folsom, & Kenneth M. Price, Editors. (https://whitmanarchive.org/literary-manuscripts).

My deep thanks to Joseph Donahue for his friendship and support across our many years of knowing one another. I am especially grateful in this instance for his intensive research that alerted me to the existence of the Whitman archive and provided me with access to materials that set this poem on its initial course. I am indebted as well to his social media postings of 19th c. artists and their artworks that gave me the cover image for this book.

For his ongoing support of and engagement with my work across multiple books, I remain deeply grateful to my editor, Tod Thilleman. His understanding of and active engagement in the drafting and revision of this book, one that arrived in his email box in multiple forms across several weeks, were decisive in my being able to see my way to completing this book. He remains a trusted first reader of my work and a valued friend, without whom much that I've accomplished across the last decade as a poet would not have been possible in the forms in which it's appeared.

Finally, to my wife, Monica Jacobe, I owe her as always more than these or any words can provide by way of acknowledgment and gratitude. Her reading and careful commenting on this book at a late stage of its drafting made all the difference to its structure and re-envisioned authorial center. This book, like so many I've written, couldn't have come into the world without her care, encouragement, and guidance.

ANDREW MOSSIN grew up in Washington, D.C. and lived in New York City for several years before moving to the Philadelphia region in the late 1980's. He is the author of numerous books of poetry, most recently, *Black Trees*; a collection of critical essays, *Male Subjectivity and Poetic Form in "New American" Poetry*, and a memoir, *A Son from the Mountains*. His edited collection of essays, *Thinking with the Poem: Essays on the Poetry and Poetics of Rachel Blau DuPlessis*, was published in 2024 by the University of New Mexico Press. He is currently collaborating with Monica Jacobe on a book of essays on the work of the visual artist and photographer William Christenberry. He lives in Doylestown, PA.

www.ingramcontent.com/pod-product-compliance
Lightning Source LLC
Chambersburg PA
CBHW020407130626
46549CB00006B/2468